# Contents

This guide book is in four sections:

A recommended tour of the cathedral

The history of St Paul's

The heritage of a nation

The cathedral today

# A recommended tour of the cathedral

St Paul's is more than a great religious centre and an architectural gem. As the cathedral of the capital city of the United Kingdom, it is the spiritual focus for the nation.

This is where people and events of special importance to the country are celebrated, mourned and commemorated. Royal weddings, state funerals and thanksgivings have all taken place at St Paul's, while hundreds of memorials in the church pay tribute to famous statesmen, soldiers, artists, doctors and writers and mark the valuable contributions to national life made by many ordinary men and women.

The present St Paul's was built between 1675 and 1710, after its predecessor was destroyed in a fire. It is the fifth cathedral to stand on the hill that dominates the ancient City of London, constantly reminding this commercial centre of the spiritual dimension of life.

This message was one that the five successive monarchs who oversaw the building of the cathedral were keen to emphasise. As Supreme Governors of the Church, they were determined that the leading church of their capital should be as beautiful and imposing as their private palaces.

Over the centuries, the cathedral has changed to reflect shifting tastes and attitudes. Decoration has been added and removed, services have been updated, different areas have been put to new uses.

Throughout, it has remained a busy, working church, where millions of people from around the world have worshipped. It is a living symbol of the city and the nation it serves and a lasting monument to the glory of God.

# The Nave

**The nave is the long central section of the cathedral that leads to the dome. It is a public and ceremonial space, designed for congregations at large services.**

• The Great West Door is nine metres high. It is now used only on ceremonial occasions. • There are three chapels at this end of the cathedral – All Souls' and St Dunstan's in the north aisle and the Chapel of the Order of St Michael and St George in the south aisle.

*For more information, see pages 20~23*

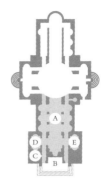

A – The nave
B – Great West Door
C – All Souls' Chapel
D – St Dunstan's Chapel
E – Chapel of St Michael and St George

B  Looking from the Great West Door towards the dome and high altar

## *Memorials in the Nave*

**The tradition of erecting memorials to famous people began at the end of the 18th century and continues today.**

• Among the memorials in the nave is one to the fire-watchers who guarded the cathedral during World War II. • A monument to one of Britain's greatest soldiers and statesmen, the Duke of Wellington, is on the north side of the nave. Wellington died in 1852 but his monument was not completed until 1912, when the figure on horseback was unveiled.

*For more information, see page 20*

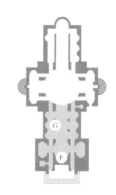

F – Fire-watchers' memorial
G – Duke of Wellington's memorial

G  The Duke of Wellington's monument

REMEMBER
MEN AND WOMEN
OF SAINT PAULS WATCH
WHO BY THE GRACE OF GOD
SAVED THIS CATHEDRAL
FROM DESTRUCTION
IN WAR
1939-1945

F  Memorial to the St Paul's Watch

## The Dome

**St Paul's is built in the shape of a cross, with the dome crowning the intersection of the arms.**

• It is one of the largest cathedral domes in the world, 111.3 metres high. It weighs approximately 65,000 tonnes and is supported by eight pillars.

*For more information, see pages 26~27*

(A) The dome and Whispering Gallery

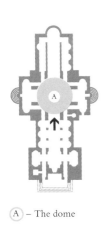

(A) – The dome

(A) Detail from the dome paintings

## *Decoration in the Dome*

**Between the arches are mosaics of prophets and saints, which were installed between 1864 and 1888.**

• The murals in the dome were created between 1715 and 1719 by court painter Sir James Thornhill and feature scenes from the life of St Paul.

*For more information, see pages 26~27 and 32*

(A) One of the dome mosaics

# The Quire

**The quire is at the east of the cathedral's cross-shape. This is where the choir and clergy – the priests – normally sit during services.**

• The quire was the first part of the cathedral to be built and consecrated.

• The choir stalls on both sides of the chancel feature delicate carvings by Grinling Gibbons, whose work is seen in many royal palaces and great houses. • The Bishop's throne, or *cathedra*, is on the south side. A cathedral takes its name from the Bishop's chair.

*For more information, see page 29*

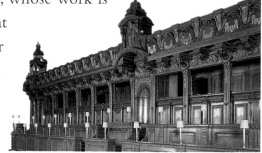

(B) The choir stalls

## The Organ

**The organ was installed in 1695 and has been rebuilt several times.**

• Its case, carved by Grinling Gibbons, is one of the cathedral's greatest artefacts. • The third largest organ in the UK, it has 7,189 pipes, five keyboards and 138 organ stops.

*For more information, see page 29*

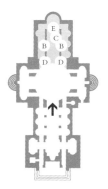

(B) – The choir stalls
(C) – The *cathedra*
(D) – The organ
(E) – The high altar

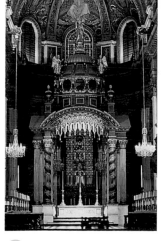

(D) The organ

## The High Altar

**Originally, the cathedral had a simple table for an altar.**

• The present high altar dates from 1958 and is made of marble and carved and gilded oak. It features a magnificent canopy based on a sketch by Wren. • It replaces a large Victorian marble altar and screen, which were damaged by a bomb in World War II.

(E) The high altar

*For more information, see page 30*

## Quire Mosaics

**Wren wanted to decorate the interior of the dome with mosaics but the cathedral authorities felt these were too lavish.**

• By the 19th century, attitudes had changed and Queen Victoria complained that the cathedral was 'Most dreary, dingy and undevotional'. • The quire mosaics were designed and installed between 1891 and 1904. • They are made in the Byzantine style, with irregular cubes of glass set at angles, so they sparkle. • They feature scenes from the creation of the world and other Bible stories.

A A detail from a quire mosaic

*For more information, see page 32*

A – Quire mosaics

## The North Transept

**The short, central arms of the cathedral's ground-plan are called transepts.**

D *The Light of the World*

B – Middlesex Chapel
C – Marble font
D – *The Light of the World*

• William Holman Hunt's painting *The Light of the World* dominates the north transept. It dates from around 1900 and is the third version that Hunt painted. • The figure of Christ knocking on a door that opens from inside suggests that God can only enter our lives if we invite Him in. • Regular services are held here in the Middlesex Chapel. • The flags are the colours of the Middlesex Regiment – the empty pole belongs to a flag that was lost during World War II. • The urn-like Italian marble font dates from 1727.

*For more information, see page 33*

C The marble font

6

# The Ambulatory

**The ambulatory is the walkway around the east end of the cathedral.**

• The mosaics in the aisles on either side of the quire feature figures of angels, a griffin (north side) and a bishop's mitre with the arms of the City of London (south side). • Several of the designs show partial nudity – something rarely seen in Anglican church decoration.

*For more information, see page 34*

G   The ambulatory mosaics

## *The North Quire Aisle*

**The wrought-iron gates were designed by the French master metalworker Jean Tijou, who was responsible for most of the decorative metalwork in the cathedral.**

• The sculpture of *Mother and Child* is by Henry Moore, who is commemorated in the crypt.
• The memorial to modern martyrs honours Anglicans who have died for their faith since 1850.

*For more information, see page 34*

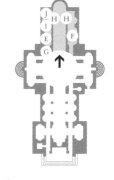

E – North quire aisle
F – South quire aisle
G – The ambulatory
H – Tijou gates
I – *Mother and Child*
J – Memorial to modern martyrs

I   Henry Moore's *Mother and Child*        H   The Tijou gates

## American Memorial Chapel

**This chapel occupies the apse – the recess behind the high altar.**

• It honours American servicemen and women who died in World War II, and was dedicated in 1958. • The roll of honour contains the names of more than 28,000 Americans who gave their lives while on their way to, or stationed in, the United Kingdom during World War II. It is kept in front of the chapel's altar.

(A) The roll of honour

• The three chapel windows date from 1960. They feature themes of service and sacrifice, while the insignia around the edges represent the American states and the US armed forces. • The limewood panelling incorporates a rocket – a tribute to America's achievements in space.

*For more information, see page 34*

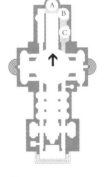

(A) – American Memorial Chapel

(A) – The roll of honour

(B) – Virgin and child

(C) – John Donne's effigy

(A) The American Memorial Chapel

## South Quire Aisle

**This aisle contains a statue of the Virgin and Child, which was once part of the Victorian altar screen, and the effigies of two Bishops of London.**

• There is also a marble effigy of John Donne – a Dean of the cathedral and one of Britain's finest poets, who died in 1631. • It is one of the few effigies to have survived the Great Fire of London – scorch marks can be seen on its base.

*For more information, see page 34*

(C) John Donne

D The monument to Admiral Lord Nelson

# The South Transept

**Admiral Nelson's monument shows Britain's greatest naval hero – who died at the Battle of Trafalgar in 1805 – leaning on an anchor.**

• His monument features a handsome lion, a symbol that means the person commemorated died in battle. • Other memorials commemorate the landscape painter JMW Turner and the explorer Captain Robert Scott, who died returning from the South Pole in 1912.

• There are three death's heads over the entrance to the crypt, where the dead are laid to rest.

*For more information, see page 33*

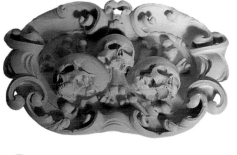
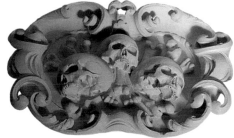

G The three death's heads

# Galleries

**On the inside of the dome, 259 steps up from floor level, is the Whispering Gallery, where a whisper against the wall can be heard on the opposite side, more than 32 metres away.**

• Above the Whispering Gallery is the Stone Gallery and, higher still, the Golden Gallery – 378 and 530 steps from the ground respectively. Both the Stone and the Golden Galleries run round the exterior of the dome and give panoramic views of London.

• The stairway to the galleries is at the junction between the south transept and the nave.

D = Nelson's monument
E = JMW Turner memorial
F = Captain Scott memorial
G = Crypt entrance
H = Galleries entrance

*For more information, see page 27*

H View from the Whispering Gallery

# The Crypt

**The crypt is the burial chamber of the cathedral. In 1936, burials in public buildings were banned except under special circumstances.**

• Unusually, the crypt of St Paul's runs the whole length of the building. • Sir Christopher Wren, architect of St Paul's, is buried in the south aisle at the east end of the crypt.

• Beside Wren's tomb is a stone bearing his architect's mark. He is surrounded by the tombs and memorials of his family. • In the same section of the crypt are many tombs and memorials of artists, scientists and musicians.

• They include the painters Sir Joshua Reynolds and Sir John Everett Millais; the scientist Sir Alexander Fleming, who discovered penicillin; the composer Sir Arthur Sullivan (of Gilbert & Sullivan); and the sculptor Henry Moore.

*For more information, see pages 36~37*

H  Bust of Sir Christopher Wren

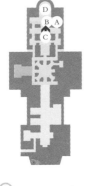

A – Wren's tomb
B – Memorials to figures in the arts
C – Memorials to figures in the sciences
D – OBE Chapel

A  Sir Christopher Wren's tomb

## OBE Chapel

**Also at the east end of the crypt is the OBE Chapel. It was dedicated to the Order of the British Empire in 1960.**

• The glass panels feature the present sovereign, scenes from the Commonwealth, commerce and the royal founders of the Order.

• Banners hanging from the ceiling represent members of the Royal Family.

*For more information, see pages 36~37*

D  The OBE Chapel

## The heart of the Crypt

**The Duke of Wellington's casket, in a chamber leading to the centre of the crypt, was so large that it had to be lowered through a hole in the cathedral floor.**

E    The Duke of Wellington's casket

• Directly under the dome lies Admiral Nelson. His casket was originally made for King Henry VIII's Lord Chancellor, Cardinal Wolsey. • Nelson's body was pickled in alcohol for the journey home from Trafalgar. • These two great men are surrounded by memorials to others who died in conflict, including those who fell in Gallipoli, Korea, the South Atlantic and the Gulf. • Florence Nightingale, George Washington and Lawrence of Arabia are also commemorated in this part of the crypt.

*For more information, see pages 38~39*

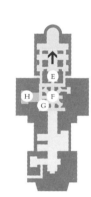

E  – Wellington's tomb
F  – Nelson's tomb
G  – Memorials
H  – The treasury area

F    Admiral Lord Nelson's casket

## The Treasury

**This area houses the treasures of the cathedral and other London churches. These include effigies from the previous St Paul's, silver, textiles and models of the building and its predecessors.**

*For more information, see page 40*

H    Embroidered Jubilee cope of 1977

H    Ceremonial items in the treasury

# The history of St Paul's

Cathedrals have always played more than one role in the communities they serve. Their central purpose is to bring people closer to God, but over the centuries they have served as a focal point for trade, as fortresses and sanctuaries in times of war, and as vast status symbols – reflections of the wealth and power of the region in which they stand.

These functions take on an additional significance for St Paul's, the cathedral of the capital city and, by extension, of the nation. The present building is also the first cathedral to have been built since the creation of the Church of England in 1534, when religion was brought under the direct control of the monarch.

In England, the Pope's refusal to grant Henry VIII a divorce from his first wife became the trigger for a reformation that linked Church and State inextricably under the leadership of the monarch, who is also Defender of the Faith.

The Church today belongs to the people of the nation. For example, every citizen can be married or have a funeral service in his or her parish church; clergy (priests) can marry couples without the presence of a civil official; and the General Synod, the Church of England's governing body, is the only organisation outside Parliament that has the power to legislate.

Cathedrals are perhaps the ultimate reflection of this inclusiveness. Unlike parish churches, which exist to minister to the people of the local area in which they stand, they are a route to God for the larger community – a place of celebration and mourning where feelings can be shared and the sheer scale and beauty of the architecture, services and music allow visitors to experience the serenity and spirituality that are an essential counterpoint to the bustle of everyday life.

# AD604 ~ The first St Paul's

St Paul's overlooks the City of London – the heart of the capital, where the first major settlements were established. The City covers just one square mile and is almost a state within a state, clinging proudly to its status and traditions.

There were even plans in the Middle Ages to run the City of London as a commune, separate from the rest of the country. As a result, London virtually governed itself for some years. Even today, the Queen has to ask the Lord Mayor's formal permission when she wants to enter the City.

There have been churches and religious monuments on the site of St Paul's since Roman times. Wren recorded that, when excavations for his building began: 'We discovered Quantities of Urns, broken Vessels and Pottery-ware.... Graves of several Ages and Fashions in Strata, or Layers of Earth, one above the other.... manifestly shew'd a great Antiquity from the British and Roman Times.'

In 604, the first Christian cathedral dedicated to St Paul was built on the site, for Mellitus, Bishop of the East Saxons. This wooden building burned down in 675 and was rebuilt 10 years later, only to be destroyed by Vikings in 962. A new church was then built in stone.

# 1087 ~ Old St Paul's

Following a fire in the City in 1087, the church had to be rebuilt again. The Norman French, who had recently conquered Britain, were determined to create the longest Christian church in the world. It was finished in 1240 but enlargement work began less than 20 years later and lasted until 1314. The cathedral was finally consecrated in 1300 – more than 200 years after it was started.

The body of the building was made of stone. The roof, however, was mainly wooden, because stone would have been too heavy to support. This choice of highly inflammable material was to have unfortunate consequences for Old St Paul's when the Great Fire of London broke out, more than 300 years later.

Over the centuries, the Norman cathedral gradually fell into disrepair. After three investigations were commissioned in the early 17th century, restoration finally began in 1633 under the direction of the architect Inigo Jones, who was also responsible for the Banqueting House at Whitehall.

The nave and transepts were refaced in Portland stone in a classical style and the west front was remodelled with a portico of noble proportions. But in 1642 the English Civil War put a stop to further work on what was now the most important classical building in the country.

During the republic – then known as the Commonwealth - which followed the execution of Charles I in 1649, the country became less respectful towards the established Church. Many places of worship became run down and Old St Paul's was no exception. Horses were stabled in the chancel, the nave was used as a marketplace and a road ran through the transepts. One observer even recorded the 'stately Portico... being converted to Shops for Seamstresses, and other Trades'.

When the monarchy was restored in 1660, the new King, Charles II, threw out the traders and began to return the scarred cathedral to its former status. In 1662, the quire was fitted out for services while the rest of the building was repaired. A year later, a Royal Commission was set up to examine the state of the building and Christopher Wren was asked to prepare a plan for the restoration.

Wren's plan was accepted in August 1666. But before he had a chance to start work, the Great Fire intervened.

A 1650 view of London showing Old St Paul's (on the left) without its spire, which was destroyed by lightning.

# 1666 ~ The Fire of London

The blaze started on 2 September and destroyed two-thirds of the City of London. It burned for four days and nights, destroying 13,200 houses and 87 parish churches, as well as Old St Paul's. Miraculously, fewer than 20 people lost their lives.

The diarist John Evelyn, one of the commissioners for the repair of the old cathedral, visited on 7 September and mourned its devastation. 'Thus lay in ashes the most venerable Churche, one of the antientest Pieces of early Piety in the Christian World,' he wrote sadly.

Charles II and the Lord Mayor quickly appointed a new commission to organise the reconstruction of the City and, just nine days after the start of the fire, Wren produced a plan. It was a celebration of light, with streets radiating out from key buildings and squares like rays from the sun. The plan also incorporated a design for a new cathedral, featuring golden stone and a luminous interior with clear glass windows and gold paintwork.

Unfortunately for Wren, the City's occupants – who needed places to live and work as soon as possible – began rebuilding almost at once. His plan never came to fruition.

# Sir Christopher Wren

Wren was one of the most extraordinary figures of his time. Although he is now best-known as an architect, he was also an astronomer, a scientist and such a talented mathematician that Sir Isaac Newton – the man who discovered gravity – ranked him as one of the world's three leading geometricians.

Throughout his life, he produced a steady stream of inventions, ranging from a pneumatic engine and an instrument that would copy handwriting to a method of fortifying port wine and a machine for knitting nine pairs of stockings simultaneously.

## The original St Paul's

This is how the first Christian church dedicated to St Paul might have looked.

## Old St Paul's

Old St Paul's is built on a magnificent scale. The immense spire becomes a familiar landmark.

## The Great Fire of London

The blaze, which starts in a bakery in Pudding Lane, devastates 430 acres of the capital. Charles II personally contributes more than £2,000 towards rebuilding St Paul's.

**AD314** ~ Restitutus becomes the first Bishop of London. The site of his cathedral is unknown.

**675** ~ The first cathedral is burned down.

**962** ~ The cathedral is rebuilt following Viking ransacking.

**1310** ~ Work is finally completed on St Paul's, more than 200 years after it began.

**1561** ~ Queen Elizabeth I contributes to repairs after lightning strikes the cathedral.

**1668** ~ Wren is commissioned to produce a new design for St Paul's Cathedral.

**AD604**
The first St Paul's Cathedral is built.

**1087**
Old St Paul's is built in a grand Norman style.

**1666**
The Great Fire of London destroys Old St Paul's.

His lasting fondness for Oxford, where he studied at Wadham College and was Professor of Astronomy from 1661–1673, is reflected in the great buildings he created there, including the Sheldonian Theatre, St John's College and Tom Tower at Christ Church.

At Cambridge, he designed Pembroke and Emmanuel College chapels and Trinity College library. For royalty and the state, his commissions included the Greenwich Observatory and Greenwich Hospital, Chelsea Hospital, and extensive work at Hampton Court Palace and Kensington Palace.

But his great passion was for the City of London, where he designed many of the replacements for the churches destroyed in the Great Fire. Perhaps his fascination with religious buildings is explained by his definition of the purpose of his work. 'Architecture,' he once explained, 'aims at eternity.'

# 1668 ~ The demolition of the old cathedral

Temporary repairs were made to Old St Paul's, but the structure was fundamentally unsound. Finally, in 1668, Wren was asked to produce a design for a new building. 'What we are to do next is the present Deliberation, in which you are so absolutely and indispensably necessary to us that we can do nothing… without you,' the Dean, William Sancroft, wrote in desperation.

Demolition of the old cathedral began the same year. Wren, as the Surveyor to the King's Works, was in charge and initially took the experimental step of using gunpowder. Like many new techniques, it was not easy to control and neighbours complained furiously about noise and damage, so Wren resorted to a battering ram instead.

The writer Samuel Pepys noted in his diary on 26 August 1668: 'It is strange to see with what speed the people imployed do pull down Paul's steeple – and with what ease.'

## Sir Christopher Wren

One of the most accomplished and successful of English architects, Wren plays an important part in establishing the classical style in 17th century Britain.

## The approved design

When Charles II approves the Warrant Design, he includes an important clause allowing Wren to modify the plan and engage craftsmen as he sees fit.

## Building the new cathedral

The construction of the cathedral takes 35 years and spans the reigns of five monarchs: Charles II, James II, William III and Mary II, and Queen Anne.

**1669** ~ Wren's first design for the new cathedral is rejected.

**1674** ~ Wren, frustrated by all the delays, works on his third design.

**1697** ~ The first service is held on 2 December in the quire, the part of the building where construction began.

**1709** ~ St Paul's introduces charges to visitors.

### 1673
Wren's second plan and Great Model are abandoned.

### 1675
Wren's Warrant Design is given royal approval.

### 1698
The structure reaches the height of the Whispering Gallery and work begins on the dome.

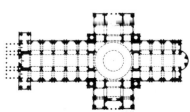

# 1669-1675 ~ The designs

Wren produced his first design in 1669. It was rejected, on the grounds that it was too foreign and insufficiently traditional.

In 1673, Charles II commissioned rebuilding work using Wren's second design as a guide. This plan was based on the shape of a Greek cross – with all four arms of equal length – and was Wren's personal favourite.

The King also commissioned a model, now known as the Great Model and on show in the Trophy Room at St Paul's, so there would be an 'unchangeable rule and direction' for the work.

But this design had to be abandoned, too. On a practical level, it could not be built in stages and the authorities did not have enough money put aside to pay for all the work at once. The other problem lay with the priests, who had old-fashioned tastes and insisted that a cathedral should follow the conventional pattern of a Latin cross – with one section, the nave, longer than the rest.

By this time, Wren was becoming extremely irritated by the criticisms and delays. He eventually produced a third design, which became known as the Warrant Design when it was given royal approval on 14 May 1675. This version featured a dome, to satisfy Wren, set on a Latin cross, to please the priests.

Having made this compromise, the architect was determined not to bow to further pressure. His son wrote: 'The Surveyor resolved to make no more Models, or publickly expose his Drawings, which (as he had found by Experience) did but lose Time, and subjected his Business many Times to incompetent Judges.'

Wren felt entitled to alter the design himself, however. When the King gave him freedom to 'make some variations, rather ornamental, than essential, as from Time to Time he should see proper' he took full advantage, changing the proportions of the building and abandoning the idea of putting a spire on top of the dome.

## The completed St Paul's

Towards the end of the project, Wren begs Queen Anne to intervene so that he can 'finish the said building in such manner...as shall be approved by your majesty'. He receives sharp criticism in return.

## Admiral Horatio Nelson

The great naval hero is brought home in the coffin he kept in his cabin. His body is taken to St Paul's by barge.

## Duke of Wellington

Around 500 workmen prepare the cathedral for the Duke's funeral. Their tasks include festooning the interior with black cloth.

**1723** ~ Sir Christopher Wren dies, aged 91. During his final years, he regularly returned to the cathedral to sit and contemplate his masterpiece.

**1810** ~ A daring robbery results in St Paul's losing most of its ceremonial gold and silver.

**1710**
The new cathedral is completed.

**1806**
A funeral service is held for Admiral Lord Nelson.

**1852**
The funeral of the Duke of Wellington.

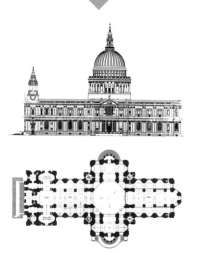

16

# 1675–1710 ~ The birth of new St Paul's

The first building contracts were confirmed in July 1675. Just 35 years later the cathedral was finished, making it the first English cathedral to be completed in the lifetime of the original architect. This speed was even more remarkable because there was a shortage of skilled labour in the aftermath of a plague which had ravaged the country in 1665.

Despite this, Wren gathered leading artists and craftsmen to work on the building. He took an active role, personally hiring and supervising workers, scrutinising the accounts and visiting the site every Saturday.

Even so, some people felt that progress was too slow. In 1697, they put pressure on Wren by persuading Parliament to suspend half his salary until the building was finished.

The perimeter walls were begun at once and the work took place behind screens, partly to hide the changes Wren was making to the approved design, but also so nobody could see the building until it was complete – unless they paid.

St Paul's has been charging tourists for entry since 1709. Indeed, a temporary suspension of the two-pence entry fee in the 19th century resulted in mayhem, according to one observer.

'In less than an hour, between 2,000 and 3,000 people entered the church, many of them of the lowest description with their hats on, laughing, talking and making uproar totally incompatible with any idea of religion,' he wrote.

Even with charges, he added, 'we see beggars, men with burdens, women knitting, parties eating luncheon, dogs, children playing, loud laughing and talking, and every kind of scenery incompatible with the solemnity of worship.'

Entrance fees did not pay for the building itself. This was funded by a special tax on coal coming into the Port of London, which was levied to finance the rebuilding of the

## Royal thanksgiving

In 1872, a royal procession and service celebrating the Prince of Wales' recovery from illness attracts 13,000 people.

## Silver Jubilee

The cathedral is again the focus for jubilee festivities when George V celebrates 25 years on the throne.

## World War II

Many buildings are damaged by bombs, including St Paul's, which is hit in 1940 and 1941.

1901 ~ A memorial service for the Queen is held at the same time as her burial at Windsor.

1939 ~ The St Paul's Fire Watch is re-formed to help City firemen fight the first fire bombs of World War II.

1944 ~The cathedral bells, silent earlier in the war, ring out to celebrate the liberation of Paris.

1897
Queen Victoria's Diamond Jubilee service.

1935
King George V's Silver Jubilee service.

1940
The cathedral is the target for a bombing raid during the Blitz.

City after the Great Fire. According to the cathedral accounts, the total cost of new St Paul's was £738,845 5 shillings 2 ½ d – approximately £50 million in modern terms.

# 1697 ~ The first service

Although the cathedral was completed in 1710, parts of it were in use up to 13 years earlier. The first section to be finished was the quire, which was opened for worship on 2 December 1697.

One onlooker commented: 'I Went to Paules to see the Choire now finished... The pulling out of the Formes [benches], like drawers from under the stalles, is very ingenious.'

The first service was a thanksgiving for peace, following the end of a war between England and France. Bishop Henry Compton's sermon included the apt words: 'I was glad when they said unto me, let us go into the House of the Lord.'

Pictures of this and later services show the congregation sitting high up in the quire stalls. They faced the pulpit, which was on wheels so that it could be moved to suit different services and sizes of congregation.

# A sad conclusion

Towards the end of the project, Wren's plans were frequently ignored. In 1711, he complained to Queen Anne that two important tasks, the decoration of the dome and the construction of the fence around the churchyard, had been taken out of his hands. He demanded the balance of his salary – and got a sharp criticism of his work along with his money.

Later, there was an even greater storm when a stone balustrade was erected around the external walls and Wren ceased to have any great influence over the fitting out of the cathedral. Even so, he returned regularly until his death at the age of 91 in 1723 to sit under the dome and contemplate his masterpiece.

## The Festival of Britain

Optimism fills the country as the Festival begins.

## Sir Winston Churchill

The great politician is the last person to receive a state funeral at the cathedral.

## Birthday celebrations

The Queen Mother's 80th birthday service is watched on television by millions of people.

1945 ~ Ten simple services are held to mark the end of the war in Europe. An estimated 35,000 people attend.

1964 ~ Human rights campaigner Martin Luther King preaches at St Paul's on his way to Oslo to collect the Nobel Peace Prize.

1968 ~ St Paul's reflects the mood of the Swinging Sixties by holding a Festival of Youth, featuring pop singer Mary Hopkin.

1980 ~ A service is held to honour the 80th birthday of the Queen Mother, who is given a silver medallion of St Paul's to mark the occasion.

1951
King George VI launches the Festival of Britain from St Paul's.

1965
The funeral of Sir Winston Churchill.

1977
A service is held to mark Queen Elizabeth II's Silver Jubilee.

# A tradition of public service

The thanksgiving service of 1697 was only the first event of national importance to be held in the new cathedral.

St Paul's has been the focus of public mourning for heroes including Admiral Nelson, the Duke of Wellington and Winston Churchill. Nelson, who was brought by barge to the cathedral, was so popular that the sailors who carried his body ripped up the flag covering his coffin for souvenirs. In honour of Wellington's funeral, the cathedral was lit by gas for the first time.

The cathedral has also provided a backdrop for happier occasions, including many thanksgiving services. In 1789 a service was held to celebrate George III's return to good health following a bout of mania; similarly, the recovery of Edward, Prince of Wales, after a severe illness was acknowledged in 1872.

Twenty-five years later, a service was held to commemorate Queen Victoria's 60th year on the throne – her Diamond Jubilee. The sermon was given on the cathedral steps while the 78-year-old queen sat nearby in her open carriage. In 1977, Queen Elizabeth II celebrated her Silver Jubilee at St Paul's.

Many thanksgiving services have been held to mark the end of Britain's involvement in armed conflict, including the recent Falklands and Gulf crises. There have also been regular events in the cathedral's calendar, such as the annual festival for charity-educated children which took place throughout the 19th century. Yearly services for members of the City guilds – trade associations – have a history stretching back 1,000 years.

Today, the cathedral is perhaps most closely associated with the marriage of Charles, Prince of Wales, and Lady Diana Spencer in 1981 in a ceremony that was watched on television by 750 million people around the world. The couple's choice of St Paul's – the nation's greatest church – rather than the monarch's own Westminster Abbey was a symbol of their mission to become the people's prince and princess.

## Royal wedding

Charles' and Diana's was the first royal wedding at St Paul's since 1501, when Arthur Tudor married Catherine of Aragon.

## Thanksgiving

The Queen and 17 members of the Royal Family remember World War II.

## Tercentenary celebrations

Festivities include musical performances and readings. There is also a special service, held in the presence of the Queen and attended by 3,000 people.

**1992** ~ The Queen Mother attends the 40th anniversary celebrations of the Friends of St Paul's.

**1996** ~ Fragments of Inigo Jones' splendid portico are discovered by archaeologists, 330 years after the Great Fire.

**1997** ~ The year ends on a high note when Dame Kiri Te Kanawa sings in the cathedral at Christmas.

**1981**
The marriage of Charles, Prince of Wales, to Lady Diana Spencer.

**1995**
A 50th anniversary service for the end of World War II in Europe.

**1997**
The 300th anniversary of St Paul's Cathedral.

# The heritage of a nation

The sheer scale and grandeur of St Paul's can be overwhelming. But behind every block of stone, wood carving, mosaic or monument lies a story of human skill, passion, tragedy or triumph. This section looks in greater depth at the cathedral and the people who have contributed to its development.

## The Nave

Over the years, St Paul's has seen many changes, but a modern visitor's first sight of the interior is much as the architect, Sir Christopher Wren, intended it to be three centuries ago – an unobstructed view of the cathedral's entire length.

In Wren's day, the Great West Door was the main entrance to the building. Now the door is rarely used, but it remains as it was in the early 18th century – with the exception of a few dents reputedly received in a riot. Made of oak and limewood, each leaf of the double door is estimated to weigh approximately two tonnes. Even so, it is secured by a single bolt that runs its entire length.

Among the cathedral's 300 memorials is a splendid monument to the Duke of Wellington, who died in 1852. Although Wellington was Prime Minister from 1828 to 1830, he is best known for his military achievements, in particular the defeat of Napoleon at Waterloo in 1815.

After his death, 13,000 mourners packed into St Paul's – nowadays the Fire Brigade sets a limit of 2,500 people in the building. Unfortunately, the Duke was late for his own funeral. His hearse, a carriage decorated with war trophies and weighing 18 tonnes, was so heavy that the horses could not pull it up the hill to the cathedral. Sailors were summoned from the nearby Pool of London to push it the rest of the way, establishing the tradition of sailors attending the gun carriage at state funerals.

Many other military figures are remembered in the aisles around the nave, including the 33,000 members of the Merchant Navy and fishing fleets who were killed in World War II, and Major General Charles Gordon, who became known as Gordon of Khartoum after he was murdered in 1885 following a 10-month siege of the Sudanese city. His bronze effigy bears the inscription: 'He saved an empire with his warlike genius, he ruled vast provinces with justice, wisdom and power.'

Works of art include a statue of Sir Joshua Reynolds, who became the first president of the Royal Academy in 1768 and is buried in the crypt, and a memorial to the 19th century painter and sculptor Lord Leighton. This effigy includes a miniature of one of Leighton's own statues, *The Sluggard*. It is flanked by two creative muses – sculpture on the right and painting on the left.

The *Gates of Death* monument in the north aisle commemorates two successive Lords Melbourne – William, who died in 1848 and was Queen Victoria's first Prime Minister, and his diplomat brother Frederick, who died in 1853. An inscription reminds readers: 'Through the gates of death we pass to our joyful resurrection.'

Plaques bearing the names of all the Deans of St Paul's since the Norman Conquest in 1066 and the Bishops of London since 314 are located in the north aisle and south aisle respectively. The first Bishop of London is recorded as Restitutus, but the site of his cathedral remains a mystery. After Restitutus there is a gap of nearly three centuries when London became a pagan city after the Romans left Britain. No other Bishop was recorded until 604.

*This page*
The Duke of Wellington's monument

*Opposite page*
Looking towards the dome and high altar

# Chapel of St Michael and St George

This chapel was originally the consistory court – the place where the Bishop sat in judgment over the clergy, or priests. It became a temporary studio for the construction of Wellington's monument between 1858 and 1878.

The monument was designed circa 1856 by the English artist Alfred Stevens, who spent most of the last 20 years of his life working on it. His pupil, Hugh Stannus, completed the main structure in 1878, three years after Stevens' death. In 1901, a third artist, John Tweed, started working on the crowning figure of the Duke on his war horse Copenhagen. This was finally added to the monument in 1912 – 60 years after Wellington's death.

The chapel housed Wellington's memorial until 1894. It was then used as a baptistry – the place where people are formally initiated into Christianity. In 1906, after refurbishment, the chapel was dedicated to the Order of St Michael and St George, an organisation founded in 1818 to honour those who have distinguished themselves overseas and in foreign affairs.

Both St Michael and St George are represented in the chapel. A statue of St George features in the screen behind the altar, while the sculpture below it shows St Michael trampling on the seven deadly sins. The artist, Edwin Russell, chose a bear to signify anger, a wolf for avarice, a serpent for envy, a vulture for gluttony, a peacock for pride and a toad for sloth. The seventh sin, lust, is a woman's face – and is said to bear a strong resemblance to the sculptor's wife.

Above the chapel's stalls are banners of current Knights of the Order. When a knight dies, the banner is returned to his family and an enamelled plaque is placed on the book-rests of the stalls as a memorial.

## Chapel of St Dunstan

This chapel, consecrated in 1699, was the second part of Wren's building to come into use, after the quire. In 1905, it was dedicated to St Dunstan, who was a Bishop of London and Archbishop of Canterbury 1,000 years ago. Before this it was known as the Morning Chapel, because the early morning office – a daily service – was said here.

The oak entrance screen was carved by one of Wren's master craftsmen and features a shield bearing the arms of the Dean and Chapter, winged cherubs and flaming urns – a symbol of eternity.

## Chapel of All Souls

Situated on the ground floor of the north-west tower, this chapel was dedicated in 1925 to the memory of Field Marshal Lord Kitchener (1850-1916) and the servicemen who died in the Great War of 1914-18 (World War I). It is also known as the Kitchener Memorial Chapel.

Kitchener was a soldier and military reformer who served in Africa and India. He restructured the British army early in World War I, but his best-known achievement was the most effective recruitment campaign in British military history, using the slogan *Your Country Needs You!* The campaign's image of Kitchener pointing a finger at viewers has often been imitated and became popular as a poster in the 1960s.

Among the chapel's artefacts are sculptures of the military saints St Michael and St George, a beautiful pietà – a sculpture of the Virgin Mary holding the body of Christ – and an effigy of Lord Kitchener. The silver-plated candlesticks on the altar are made from melted-down trophies won by the London Rifle Brigade.

*Opposite page*
The Chapel of the Order of
St Michael and St George

*This page*
Top:    The Chapel of All Souls, or
        Kitchener Memorial Chapel
*Bottom*: Chapel of St Dunstan

### THE DEVIL AND ST DUNSTAN

*According to legend, St Dunstan was a skilled blacksmith who shod the Devil with horseshoes. In return, he made Satan promise never to enter a house with a horseshoe nailed above the door. He is often shown holding the Devil, sometimes by the nose, with a pair of pliers.*

*This page*
The dome from below

*Opposite page*
Top:    Detail from Thornhill's
        dome murals
Bottom: The floor beneath
        the dome

# The Dome

Wren was determined to crown his church with a soaring dome rather than a spire, even though this was highly unusual in England during the late 17th century.

Superstition surrounded the rebuilding of the cathedral, but one incident early in its construction was taken to be a good omen.

Wren's son Christopher recorded it in his book, *Parentalia*: 'When the Surveyor… [Wren] had set out… the Dimension of the great Dome, and fixed upon the Centre; a common labourer was ordered to bring a flat Stone… to be laid for a Mark and Direction to the Masons; the Stone… happened to be a Piece of a Grave-Stone, with nothing remaining of the Inscription but the single Word in large Capitals, RESURGAM.'

The significance of the word, which means 'I shall rise again', was not lost on the architect, and it was carved on the pediment above the door of the cathedral's south transept.

Building such a large structure created complex technical problems, but Wren came up with solutions that were both ingenious and aesthetically pleasing. To get over the difficulty of joining the circular dome to the rest of the cathedral, for example, he used eight supporting arches.

Wren intended to decorate the inside of the dome in mosaic and even selected four Italian artists for the job. But, in 1709, the Cathedral Commissioners appointed the English decorative artist James Thornhill to paint it in monochrome – partly because mosaic was expensive and time-consuming and partly because such a highly decorative medium was thought too foreign and elaborate. Thornhill, who had made his name at Hampton Court Palace, began the work six years later and finished in 1719.

Thornhill based the mural on a series of pen and ink sketches of scenes from the life of St Paul. He made three sets of eight drawings and hung the various options for each scene in the dome before making his decision. One set of these pictures is still kept at St Paul's. The other two are in the Victoria & Albert Museum and the British Museum.

By the end of the 18th century, the murals were suffering the effects of the British climate and London smog. By the mid-19th century, they were nearly invisible. When a painter was employed to clean them in 1853, the damage was so bad that he ended up repainting much of the ceiling. What can be seen today is, therefore, not original, although the paintings are copied from Thornhill's designs.

## The Galleries

The dome is one of the largest in the world – comparable in size to the dome of St Peter's in Rome. To prevent it looking like a dark funnel, Wren made the inner dome significantly lower than the outside.

The Whispering Gallery runs around the interior and is 259 steps up from ground-level. It gets its name from a charming quirk in its construction, which makes a whisper against its walls audible on the opposite side.

This gallery's decorative metal railing was designed and made by the French master metalworker Jean Tijou, who also created the beautifully-wrought high altar gates. Tijou worked on some of the nation's greatest houses, including Hampton Court Palace. Unlike many artists, he could also turn his hand to practical projects. It was Tijou who made the strong iron chains used by Wren to stabilise the scaffolding around the dome.

There are two higher galleries encircling the outside of the dome – the Stone Gallery, which at 173 ft (53.4 metres) high is reached by 378 steps, and the much smaller Golden Gallery, which runs around the highest point of the outer dome, 280 ft (85.4 metres) and 530 steps from ground level.

While the dome and galleries were being built, Wren was hauled up and down in a basket at least once a week to inspect the work in progress. He was 76 by the time this work was completed in 1708 and he watched as his son placed the last stone in position.

*Opposite page*
The quire and high altar

*This page*
The organ on the south side of the quire

### ORGAN STOP

*Mendelssohn once played the organ so long after the service, and the congregation was so reluctant to leave, that cathedral staff brought the performance to an abrupt end by letting the wind out of the instrument.*

# The Quire

When the cathedral was built, it was usual for the nave and the quire to be separated by a screen. St Paul's had an elaborate screen with the organ fixed on top of it – an arrangement that Wren disliked because it obstructed the view down the church.

Over the centuries, the organ has been repositioned, rebuilt and modified several times. One of the greatest changes came in 1871, when the screen was removed and the instrument divided into two parts.

The organ was made for the cathedral by a German known as Father Schmidt and was installed in 1695 – the head organ-maker traditionally enjoyed the courtesy title of Father. Schmidt made himself unpopular with Wren by taking too long and nearly setting fire to the cathedral. He also asked for alterations in the plans to accommodate the enormous instrument, allegedly provoking Wren into snapping, 'I'll not alter my church for a box of whistles.'

One major improvement was the installation of a set of pipes known as the diapason chorus. This introduces music at the back of the cathedral, which cancels out a nine-second echo and helps the rear of the congregation to stay in harmony with people at the front.

The composers Handel and Mendelssohn both played the organ on many occasions. For Handel, the main attraction was its set of pedals, which were a rarity in the 18th century. Mendelssohn preferred the C-pedal board, which improved his renditions of Bach.

The musical historian George Burney wrote: 'Handel, after three o'clock prayers, used frequently to get himself…locked up in the church…and in the summer often stript unto his shirt, and played away until eight or nine o'clock at night.'

Although the organ has seen many changes, it retains its original case. This was carved with characteristic delicacy by the Anglo-Dutch sculptor Grinling Gibbons, who also created the exquisite decorations on the choir stalls. Gibbons is said to have received the grand sum of 33 shillings for his stall carvings – about £128 today.

'There is no instance of a man before Gibbons who gave to wood the loose and airy lightness of flowers…with the free disorder natural to each species,' wrote one commentator.

On the south of the quire is a modern carved oak and limewood pulpit, which was installed in 1964 to celebrate the 250th anniversary of the cathedral's completion.

The *cathedra*, or Bishop's throne, is also in the quire. It is lavishly decorated with flowers, leaves, garlands and winged cherubs. Within it is a high-backed chair showing the emblem of Bishop Compton, who preached at the cathedral's first service.

# High Altar

The cathedral's original altar was a simple wooden table, which was not grand enough for Victorian tastes. So, in 1888, a large, ornate altar, topped by a monumental marble screen, was installed in the centre of the quire.

It stood for little more than 50 years. A bomb hit the quire in 1940, damaging the screen, which had to be removed. After the war, the rest of the altar was also taken away.

The current high altar was installed in 1958 as both a focus for worship and a memorial from the British people to the 335,451 members of the Commonwealth who were killed in the two world wars.

Its base is made of a slab of Italian marble that weighs four tonnes and its magnificent canopy is taken from a sketch by Wren. This design was vetoed by the priests of Wren's time, who found it offensively decorative. The structure is crowned by the gilded figure of Christ with his right hand extended in blessing.

On either side of the high altar are two enormous carved candlesticks, copies of a pair commissioned by Cardinal Wolsey in the 16th century to stand with his burial casket. Before he had any need of this elaborate memorial, the Cardinal argued with King Henry VIII, who promptly confiscated both the casket and the unfinished candlesticks.

The candlesticks were completed, with the addition of Henry's own emblems – Tudor roses and the Tudor coat of arms – and were sold to a Belgian cathedral by the republican Oliver Cromwell during the 17th century. Copies also exist at St George's Chapel in Windsor Castle and at London's Victoria & Albert Museum.

The Wolsey casket was stored at Windsor Castle until Admiral Nelson's victory and death in the Battle of Trafalgar in 1805.

It was considered suitable for a national hero, so the original carved Cardinal's hat was removed from the top and replaced with a Viscount's coronet before Nelson was buried in the crypt of St Paul's.

## RESTORING THE DAMAGE

*The bomb that came through the quire roof in 1940 caused considerable damage to the east end of the cathedral, as well as to the altar. As part of the redevelopment, the American Memorial Chapel was created – financed by the British people.*

*A national appeal for funds was launched in 1945, which included a short film made by the Dean of St Paul's. The film was shown in cinemas throughout the country and afterwards members of the Women's Royal Voluntary Service collected donations.*

*More than £57,000 (equivalent to about £1.28 million today) was raised, ranging from cheques from wealthy corporations to pennies given by children in an orphanage.*

*This page*
The high altar, which is also a war memorial

*Opposite page*
Looking down the cathedral from the east end

30

THIS CHAPEL COMMEMORATES THE COMMON SACRIFICES OF
THE BRITISH AND AMERICAN PEOPLES DURING THE SECOND
WORLD WAR AND ESPECIALLY THOSE AMERICAN SERVICE MEN
WHOSE NAMES ARE RECORDED IN ITS ROLL OF HONOUR
THIS TABLET WAS UNVEILED BY H. M. QUEEN ELIZABETH II
ON 26 NOVEMBER 1958 IN THE PRESENCE OF RICHARD M. NIXON
THE VICE PRESIDENT OF THE UNITED STATES OF AMERICA

# Mosaics

During the second half of the 19th century, most of the clergy agreed that the cathedral's interior needed redecorating. In 1858, the Dean, Henry Hart Milman, wrote, '…instead of the cold, dull, unedifying, unseemly appearance of the interior, the cathedral should be made within worthy of its exterior grandeur and beauty… I would [like to] see the dome, instead of brooding like a dead weight over the area below, expanding and elevating the soul towards heaven.'

But it proved difficult to secure the necessary funding and develop a scheme that suited everybody. Various plans were submitted and discussed, including proposals to add colour to the dome murals.

Eventually, in 1864, the first mosaic was installed on the spandrels – the triangular spaces between the arches and the curve of the dome. It was designed by Alfred Stevens, who was working on Wellington's monument at the time, and shows the prophet Isaiah. Stevens designed three more spandrel mosaics, again of prophets. Another artist, George Frederick Watts, produced two further designs, showing St John and St Matthew.

Watts' design for St Matthew was later installed. But it was left to a third artist, WEF Britten, to complete the four remaining designs and two of his own, showing St Mark and St Luke – a process that took five years, from 1888 to 1893. It is a tribute to Britten's skill that all eight mosaics appear to be the work of one person.

The mosaics at the east end of the cathedral and in the four corner arches of the dome were commissioned in 1891 to complement the splendour of the new altar. They are the work of William Blake Richmond, who completed the last section in 1904.

Unlike the glass cubes that form the spandrel mosaics, which were manufactured on the island of Murano in Venice, Richmond's mosaics were made from start to finish in London. More than two centimetres of stonework was cut away so that they could be fitted.

During World War II, a section of mosaic in the squared archway above the quire was damaged by a bomb. It was repaired in 1959 with help from Italian artisans, one of whom told his granddaughter that she should look closely at the angels, if she ever went to St Paul's. When she finally arrived, she saw he had given one the face of her grandmother – and spent her visit staring up at it, weeping silently.

# The Transepts

William Holman Hunt's *The Light of the World*, in the north transept, is one of the few paintings left in St Paul's – most of the others were removed for safe-keeping during World War II and never returned. The artist, who is buried in the crypt, was one of the founders of the Pre-Raphaelite movement.

*The Light of the World* is one of the most copied pictures in the world – the artist himself painted the same subject three times.

The first version, which was painted by moonlight, is in Keble College, Oxford. Angered that the college did not intend to display it to the public, Hunt painted a second version, which is now in Manchester Civic Art Gallery. A shipowner, Charles Booth, commissioned the third version, much of which was painted by Hunt's students because the artist was, by then, in his 70s and nearly blind. Booth presented it to St Paul's in 1908.

The south transept is home to a monument to Admiral Horatio Nelson – one of Britain's most romantic heroes. Nelson went to sea for the first time at the age of 12, prompting his uncle to write: 'What has poor Horace done, who is so weak, that he…should be sent to rough it out at sea?'

The monument shows a cloak covering the area where Nelson's right arm should be – the limb was amputated after a direct hit in 1797. Three years earlier, he had lost the sight in his right eye, although, contrary to tradition, he never wore an eye-patch.

Nelson's life also featured a tragic love story. He abandoned his wife, Fanny, for the woman he called 'beloved Emma, the dear friend of my bosom' – Lady Emma Hamilton.

The lovers had a daughter, Horatia, whose birth was kept secret. Nelson made an addition to his will shortly before his last battle requesting that the nation should support his illegitimate family, 'both of whom I love as much as my own life'. The will concluded: 'These are the only favours I ask of my King and Country at this moment when I am going to fight their Battle.'

Sadly, Emma and Horatia received nothing.

### LIFTING THE LID ON THE FONT

*A font contains the water used in baptism, the ceremony that formally welcomes people into Christianity. St Paul's 18th century font was made by Francis Bird, who sculpted the relief above the cathedral's entrance. The lid is so heavy that it takes a block and tackle to lift it. A hatch – known as the Slice of Cake – makes access easier.*

*Opposite page*
Top:     Mosaics in the saucer-domes above the quire, showing scenes from God's creation of the world
Bottom:  Detail from the mosaics in the quire, showing one of the angels: 'The morning stars of the creation of the first sons of God'
*This page*
Nelson's monument

*This page*
*Top*: Tijou's Golden Gates
*Bottom*: John Donne's effigy

*Opposite page*
The American Memorial Chapel

# Ambulatory and American Memorial Chapel

The changing life and appearance of the cathedral are clearly seen in the walkway around the quire. Modern art – such as the 1984 Henry Moore sculpture *Mother and Child* in the north quire aisle – stands proudly in surroundings many centuries its senior, while the 20th century American Memorial Chapel blends into the 17th century structure of the building.

Close to Moore's sculpture are two pairs of wrought iron gates made by Jean Tijou around 1700 in the extravagant Baroque style. The Golden Gates between the aisles and the quire were part of the organ screen until the late 19th century, while the Candelabra Gates at each end of the ambulatory are in their original position.

Behind the high altar is the American Memorial Chapel – a monument to the thousands of Americans who were killed either on their way to, or while stationed in, the United Kingdom during World War II.

The idea of a central memorial was first put forward by the US Army Air Force in 1945 and the Dean of St Paul's volunteered the cathedral for its location. 'It is not for you but for us to erect that memorial,' said Lord Trenchard, chairman of the Anglo-American Commission, so the chapel became a tribute from the British people, who contributed to a national appeal for funds.

Their gratitude is recognised in the inscription that edges the marble floor: 'To the American dead of the Second World War from the people of Britain.'

During the war, a section of the quire near the proposed site of the chapel had been damaged by a bomb, so the architects were able to make quite radical changes as part of the redevelopment, including the installation of a new central stained glass window and the new high altar.

The chapel itself is packed with symbolism. For example, a pelican in the central window suggests the personal sacrifice made by the dead, so that others could live in peace and freedom.

The altar rails, designed to echo Tijou's gates, continue the theme. Between flourishes of English oak leaves, paper scrolls represent the shared cultural heritage of Britain and America, while references to the life of Moses allude to the many Jewish men who fought in the war.

Important dates are also woven into the design. These include 1607 (the foundation of the first permanent English settlement in North America, in Jamestown, Virginia), 1710 (when Wren completed the present St Paul's) and 1776 (the signing of the Declaration of Independence that established the USA).

General Eisenhower – later President Eisenhower – asked if he could provide a roll of honour, listing the men and women who are commemorated in the chapel. A 500-page illustrated manuscript was presented in 1951 and a copy of the book is available so that visitors can find the names of loved ones.

In the south aisle of the ambulatory is Dr John Donne's effigy, the only statue in St Paul's to have come through the Great Fire intact. Donne composed some of the most intricate love poems in the English language, many of them for his wife, Anne, with whom he eloped when she was only 17. 'John Donne, Anne Donne, un-done', he wrote of the scandal this caused.

After his wife's death in childbirth, he grew increasingly morbid. During his last illness, Donne insisted on wrapping himself in a sheet, to simulate a shroud, while posing for his effigy. He kept the finished figure by his bedside as a reminder of his fate.

Donne's decision was unconventional, but it meant that his image had no arms and legs to be broken when it fell into the crypt during the Great Fire or during the bombings of World War II.

# The Crypt

The floor of the crypt was originally plain earth – coffins were simply buried and a stone was placed on top. But the Victorians, who started the tradition of viewing the crypt as well as the rest of the church, decided that a proper floor was needed.

To save money – and, perhaps, the souls of the workers concerned – the cathedral authorities brought in women prisoners from Woking Gaol to lay the mosaic floor. Unsurprisingly, they were not very good at the job at first and there is a noticeable improvement in the quality of the work as they progressed through the crypt.

The Victorians also introduced a central heating system in the crypt, burning wood in braziers and then using oil as fuel. The fires warmed the air, which rose through large brass grilles to the church above. The cathedral is still heated from below today.

The entire eastern section of the crypt used to be known as St Faith's, or St Faith's under St Paul's. Until the Fire of London, St Faith's was a parish church attached to Old St Paul's and was the church of the Worshipful Company of Stationers, a booksellers' and publishers' guild. The guild still meets here in the OBE (Order of the British Empire) Chapel on special occasions.

The OBE was created in 1917 because the king, George V, wanted to be able to recognise the contribution made by women during World War I. Until then, no woman had been eligible for a decoration, although an exception had been made for Florence Nightingale, founder of modern British nursing, who was given the Order of Merit. The OBE was separated into military and civil divisions in 1918.

Today, holders of the OBE have the right to be married and to have members of their families baptised in the chapel.

Set in the chapel's ceiling is a gold shell – the emblem of St James the Great. St James died in Jerusalem but in legend his body is said to have ended up at Santiago de Compostela in north-west Spain. Pilgrims visiting Santiago would wear a cockle shell in their hair to show that they had made the journey to his resting place.

Surrounding the OBE chapel are the tombs and memorials of many celebrated figures from the arts and sciences, including Wren, who is buried in the south-east aisle. Wren did not want to be commemorated, perhaps believing his cathedral was the best monument to his life and work.

Other memorials nearby are a reminder of Wren's diverse talents. Tributes to members of the Royal Academy, an institution promoting the study of the arts, sit alongside those to fellows of its scientific counterpart, the Royal Society, of which Wren was a founder member.

Figures from the arts who are buried here include the painter and first president of the Royal Academy, Sir Joshua Reynolds. Those remembered with memorials include composer Ivor Novello; writer and caricaturist Max Beerbohm; architect Sir Edwin Lutyens; artist Sir Anthony Van Dyck; artist and poet William Blake; and landscape painter John Constable.

Memorials to scientists and others who have contributed to national life include pharmacist and philanthropist Sir Henry Wellcome; the 14th century priest and scholar John Wycliffe, who was responsible for translating the Bible into English; and Florence Nightingale.

Close to the south entrance there are tributes to war journalists, including a memorial to the man known as the father of war reporting, Sir William Howard Russell. He was the first journalist to send back live descriptions of battle scenes and made his earliest reports from the Crimean war – the conflict in which Florence Nightingale made her name.

### LOOK AROUND YOU

*Wren's son, Christopher, wrote the epitaph that appears in full on the floor under the dome and abridged over his tomb. It is in Latin and translates as: 'Beneath lies buried the founder of this church and city, Christopher Wren, who lived more than 90 years, not for himself but for the public good. Reader, if you seek his monument, look around you.'*

*Opposite page*
The OBE Chapel

*This page*
*Top:* Memorial to Florence Nightingale
*Bottom:* Wren's resting place

# National heroes

Two great military figures, the Duke of Wellington and Admiral Nelson, lie at the heart of the crypt, surrounded by tributes to others who died for their country.

In contrast to his elaborate monument in the cathedral above, Wellington rests in a simple casket made of Cornish granite. Although he was a national hero, he was not a man to glory in his victories. 'Nothing except a battle lost can be half so melancholy as a battle won,' he wrote in a despatch of 1815, the year in which he defeated Napoleon at Waterloo.

The Duke, who was known as The Iron Duke as a result of his tireless campaigning, has left a colourful list of namesakes – Wellington boots, the dish Beef Wellington and even a brand of cigars. He also coined some memorable phrases.

He gave the expression '… and another thing' to the English language and declared: 'The battle of Waterloo was won on the playing fields of Eton.' He also came up with 'circumstances over which I have no control', as well as the immortal line: 'Publish and be damned.'

The banners hanging around Wellington's tomb were made for his funeral procession. Originally, there was one for Prussia, which was removed during World War I and never reinstated.

On the walls are memorials to field marshals from World War II, including one to Sir Claude Auchinleck. At the time it was installed, Sir Claude had emigrated to Africa. Eventually an official realised that there had been no confirmation of his death and, after he had been traced, a letter of apology was sent. Sir Claude was not at all put out and sent back a reply to say so – drily pointing out that time would rectify the mistake.

Admiral Nelson lies at the centre of the crypt, directly beneath the middle of the dome. His monument includes a call to national prayer that he wrote while in view of the enemy before the Battle of Trafalgar in 1805.

It reads: 'May the Great God whom I worship Grant to my Country for the benefit of Europe in General a great and Glorious Victory, and may no misconduct in anyone tarnish it, and may humanity after Victory be the predominant feature in the British Fleet. For myself individually I commit my life to Him Who made me, and may His blessing alight on my endeavours for serving my Country faithfully. To Him I resign myself and the just cause which is entrusted to me to Defend. Amen, Amen, Amen.'

Nelson was killed in the battle, but was well prepared for this eventuality and had his coffin with him. It was made from the mast of a French ship sunk in one of his earlier victories and he kept it propped behind his desk.

His body had to be preserved for the journey home, so it was soaked in French brandy. At Gibraltar, it was transferred - still in the coffin - into a lead-lined casket and steeped in distilled wine. When the pickled remains reached England, they were put in two more coffins before being buried in the crypt, beneath Cardinal Wolsey's 16th century sarcophagus.

Many other military figures are commemorated alongside Wellington and Nelson, both individually and in groups. Close to these great leaders are poignant reminders of those who fell this century in the Boer War, Gallipoli, Korea, the South Atlantic and the Gulf.

In an aisle nearby are the tombs of Admiral Earl David Beatty and Admiral Earl John Jellicoe, who fell out over the failure of the battle of Jutland in 1916 but ended up being buried side-by-side. Close to them is a tribute to Pilot Officer William Fiske – an American who joined the British Air Force during World War II and who died in the Battle of Britain. The inscription on his memorial reads: 'An American citizen who died that England might live.'

There are also more recent memorials, including a tribute to Professor Gordon Hamilton-Fairley, who was killed by a terrorist bomb in 1975. He is remembered with the moving quotation: 'It matters not how a man dies but how he lives.'

*Opposite page*
Nelson's burial place

*This page*
Top:     Memorial to servicemen who took part in the Gallipoli campaign
Bottom:  Wellington's granite casket

# The Treasury

Over the centuries, many of the cathedral's treasures have been lost. There was one especially disastrous robbery in 1810, when much of St Paul's gold and silver was stolen. As a result, many of the precious items on display in the treasury today belong to the churches of London, who have loaned St Paul's more than 200 ceremonial vessels and accessories.

The cathedral does still occasionally add to its store of artefacts, however. The splendid Jubilee Cope, or cape, is a relatively recent acquisition, dating from 1977. It was made for a thanksgiving service in honour of the Queen's Silver Jubilee – the 25th anniversary of her coronation – where it was worn by Gerald Ellison, the Bishop of London.

The cope features the embroidered spires of 73 London churches and three Royal Peculiars – churches allied to the monarch rather than any clerical body. St Paul's is depicted in the centre of the back.

As well as the cope and other clerical robes, the treasury houses several sectional models of the dome and cathedral. There is also a representation of Old St Paul's and the cathedral today. Other artefacts include a picture of the organ in its original position on top of the screen and another of the Victorian altar screen, which was removed after World War II.

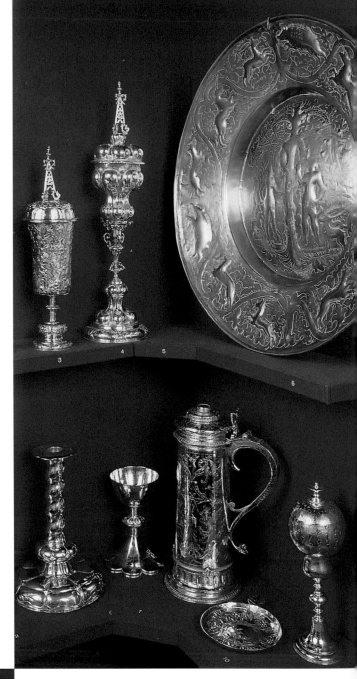

At the edge of the treasury are two effigies that pre-date the Great Fire. Although they look as if they are made of wood, they are actually stone. Originally they were painted in bright, lifelike colours, but the heat of the fire fused the paint to the surface and turned the stone the colour of ancient, polished oak.

A display near the treasury provides more detail about the Great Fire and the damage it caused. It gives an historical account of the blaze, which began in a baker's shop in Pudding Lane and destroyed two-thirds of the City of London.

# Triforium

A triforium is a gallery. The word actually means 'made of three parts' – a reference to the three sections of the cathedral formed by the central nave, the side aisles and the gallery above.

One of the delights of the triforium is the cathedral's library – a panelled room which has remained virtually unchanged since its completion in 1709. As in other, more public, parts of St Paul's, there is great attention to detail in the decoration. The stone pilasters by the windows, for instance, are carved with books and quill pens.

The library contains approximately 13,000 books, as well as shelves of sermons, pamphlets and music scores, many of which were written for the cathedral choir. These works – nearly 30,000 in total – are available to scholars by appointment.

Among the library's treasures is an illustrated Nuremberg Bible from 1649 and another dating from a century before. The earlier Bible originally belonged to Thomas Cranmer, the Archbishop of Canterbury, who helped Henry VIII to obtain his first divorce. The library's oldest work is a service book, which was written by hand more than 800 years ago and was used in Old St Paul's, while the rarest volume is a first edition of William Tyndale's New Testament of 1525 – one of only three copies left in the world.

Above the Great West Door, the Royal Trumpets and diapason chorus can be seen. The trumpets were installed in honour of the Queen's Silver Jubilee in 1977 and were so loud that she is said to have been startled. They have not been used in her presence since.

The Trophy Room is home to the surviving models of Wren's designs and facsimiles of his architectural drawings. The centrepiece is the Great Model of Wren's Greek cross design for St Paul's. This was finished in 1674 at a cost of £600 – the price of a good London house at the time. The sum is roughly equivalent to £44,350 today.

Beside the Trophy Room is a drawing of St Paul's in cross section, made during repairs to the cathedral from 1923 to 1928. There are many other pictures and sculptures in the triforium, tracing the history of St Paul's and the people whose lives it has touched.

• *Visitors wishing to take a guided tour of the triforium should telephone 0171-246 8319 to make a reservation.*

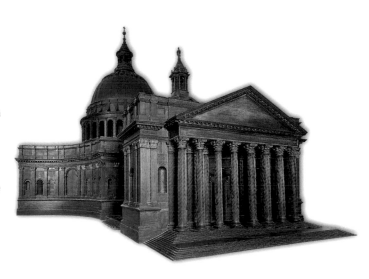

## BOOKMARKS

*An inscription over the librarian's office reads: 'Of making many books there is no end.' This is particularly appropriate now, as the entire collection is being catalogued for the first time.*

Opposite page
Top:      Some of the treasury's 200 ceremonial items
Bottom:   Silver items in the treasury collection

This page
Top:      The Great Model
Bottom:   Inside the library

# Exterior and churchyard

Wren intended St Paul's to have a single-storey entrance supported by a row of classical columns but no stones of sufficient size were available. Instead, he divided the portico into two levels, with four pairs of pillars on top and six pairs below. He also included a gallery in the portico's upper levels, reputedly hoping the Bishop of London would use it to bless the crowds below – as the Pope does in Rome.

Above the entrance is a relief showing the Conversion of St Paul to Christianity. On top of it stands the figure of St Paul himself. Both were sculpted by Francis Bird, who was responsible for much of the cathedral's exterior decoration, as well as a statue of Queen Anne, the reigning monarch at the time of the cathedral's completion. The statue gradually fell into disrepair and was replaced in 1885 by the version that stands in front of the building today.

Bird also sculpted the figures on either side of St Paul – St James on the right and St Peter on the left. These are two of a series of sculptures set around the cathedral.

There are further reliefs showing scenes from the life of St Paul in the entrance portico, as well as an 18th century graffito that says: 'JH 1701'.

The portico is flanked by twin towers, each topped with a pineapple – a symbol of peace, prosperity and hospitality. The door in the north-west tower was used to get to the Chapter House, the cathedral's administrative centre, which was built by Wren in red brick after he had finished the cathedral. The Chapter House was badly damaged by a bomb in the Blitz and was completely rebuilt in the 1950s.

The entrance in the south-west tower is known as the Dean's Door - it provides the most direct route between the Deanery and the cathedral. Bird decorated the area around the door, and commemorated the death of the Dean who had ordered the work by carving a tear on the cheek of a cherub.

Near the top of the south-west tower is the clock, which has three faces, each more than 16 ft (five metres) in diameter. It was installed by John Smith and Sons of Derby in 1893.

### THE BALLAD OF BRANDY NAN

*The fact that Queen Anne's statue faced away from St Paul's caused much comment, including this popular rhyme from the early 18th century:*

> *'Brandy Nan, Brandy Nan,*
> *They've left you in the lurch,*
> *Facing towards the gin shops,*
> *With your back towards the church.'*

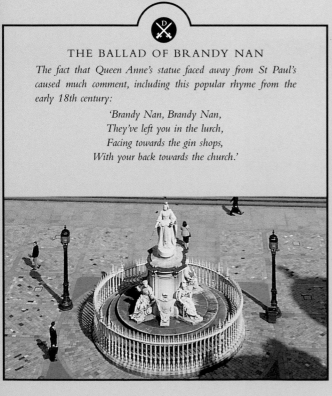

*Opposite page*
St Paul's at night

*This page*
*Top:* Bird's statue of St Paul
*Bottom:* The magnificent portico

Above the clock are Great Tom, the hour bell, and Great Paul, the largest swinging bell in Europe. Great Paul, which predates the cathedral, is sometimes called the Recall Bell because it used to be rung to call the apprentices back to work after lunch. It still strikes daily at 1pm. Great Tom strikes the hours and also marks the death of royalty and senior churchmen. It was presented to the cathedral in 1716. The north-west tower houses the remaining 12 bells, which sound the peal.

The semi-circular north transept portico is based on the entrance to the church of Santa Maria della Pace in Rome. Although Wren never visited Rome, he had seen engravings of the building.

On the south side, the main focal point is the relief above the door on the south transept pediment. This features a phoenix – a mythical bird that died in a fire and came back to life. It has a double significance, symbolising both the resurrection of Christ after the crucifixion and the building of the cathedral, which rose from the ashes of Old St Paul's.

St Paul's Cross Memorial dominates the churchyard. This column, mounted with a gilded statue of St Paul, commemorates an outdoor preaching pulpit which played an important part in London life for centuries before it was destroyed in the Great Fire of 1666.

A statue of John Wesley, the founder of Methodism, stands nearby. He regularly worshipped at St Paul's in the 18th century.

The railings on the northern perimeter of the churchyard angered Wren, who found them 'ugly, extravagant and quite unsuitable', but they are now highly valued as one of the earliest pieces of cast iron work in the country.

# The cathedral today

With at least four services every day, more than two million visitors each year, a world-famous school and choir and a variety of buildings, St Paul's is as complex as any major corporation.

Behind the stately facades, hundreds of people work in jobs as diverse as conservation, security, teaching and stonemasonry. They fall into three main groups: clergy (priests), other staff and volunteers.

Their ultimate overseers are the Dean and Chapter – five senior priests who act as the board of directors of the enterprise and are responsible for every aspect of daily organisation.

The Dean is chairman, with four canons – including the Archdeacon of London – as his board. Their primary job is to maintain the daily round of worship, with services at 7.30am, 8am, 12.30pm and 5pm. The late service, evensong, is most popular, and is often attended by as many as 300 people.

They are assisted by the College of Minor Canons, three young priests who organise and conduct services.

The Chapter have administrative roles as well as their religious duties. The Archdeacon is the chief link with the City of London and is responsible for its parishes – more than 30 of them. The other three canons, who live in houses that form part of the cathedral complex, are the Precentor, who is responsible for worship, music and the choir school; the Treasurer, who is in charge of monuments, treasures, memorials and special services; and the Chancellor, who looks after education, the library, tourism and marketing.

The Dean and Chapter meet once a fortnight to plan the running of the cathedral, delegating jobs to a staff of 158, including vergers, stewards, shop and office staff.

There are also 30 prebendaries, London priests who act as non-executive directors of St Paul's. They join the Dean and Chapter once a year on St Paul's Day – 25 January – for what is effectively an annual meeting. They are not paid, but have their own stall in the cathedral quire.

The Bishop of London plays no part in the day-to-day affairs of St Paul's, although his throne is kept there and he is regularly invited to preach and assist at special services. His principal role is the leadership and welfare of the Church in the area of London north of the Thames.

# Maintaining St Paul's

Repairing, restoring and adding to St Paul's is a continuous process that accounts for around 40 per cent of the cathedral's annual outgoings.

Remedial work is carried out according to a 25-year master plan, which is revised every five years, and involves craftspeople with a wide range of special skills, from stonemasonry and carving to scaffolding and decorating.

One major project on the dome recently involved removing the outer stone, checking, cleaning and repairing the 300-year-old wrought iron chains that hold the structure together, and putting everything back in place.

The works team also includes cleaners, electricians, security guards, plumbers and heating engineers, a painter, a gardener, a conservation expert and a draughtsman.

Conserving and modernising a great cathedral and its contents is, of course, expensive. The toilets alone cost £40,000-a-year to run and the total annual maintenance bill is around £1 million, which is covered by a combination of entrance fees, grants and external funding.

The maintenance team can tackle some jobs when the cathedral is closed but, inevitably, they often have to work alongside as many as 4,000 visitors a day, causing as little noise and disruption as possible. They down tools every hour, while prayers are said.

But St Paul's can upset even the most careful plans. In 1997, a Roman burial site was uncovered when new staff rest rooms and showers were being built in the cathedral grounds. Work had to stop while a team of archaeologists logged the remains, took photographs and removed artefacts.

Given the history of the site, such discoveries are not unusual. Human remains are always reburied in holy ground and blessed – then the maintenance work continues.

## ROCK OF AGES

*Despite the age of the cathedral buildings, it is still possible to find appropriate materials for maintenance. For example, the Portland stone used to repair the walls comes from the same quarry in Dorset used by Wren three centuries ago.*

*Opposite page*
The Dean and Chapter:
(left to right) the Reverend Canon Michael Saward, Treasurer; the Venerable George Cassidy, Archdeacon of London; the Very Reverend Dr John Moses, Dean; the Reverend Canon John Halliburton, Chancellor; and the Reverend Stephen Oliver, Precentor

*This page*
*Top:*     Restoring wood
           carvings
*Centre:*  Masons at work
*Bottom:*  Oiling the clock

# Music

Music is a crucial element of worship and life at St Paul's. Its ability to express emotion and to transcend cultural and social barriers is especially valuable in a cathedral, where there is no regular congregation and visitors from many different backgrounds and countries attend services.

The service sheet expresses its unifying influence: 'As words and music come together and enrich each other, our senses and intellects, our hearts and minds, are drawn closer to God.'

The music itself, which the 18th century composer Joseph Haydn described as the most beautiful sound he had ever heard, is the result of centuries of dedication to excellence and the hard work of many musicians. Today, these include the organist, sub-organist, assistant organist, 18 adult singers known as the Vicars Choral and around 40 choristers.

These boys are educated at the St Paul's Cathedral School. The present school has its distant origins in a song school that was founded in 604, along with the first St Paul's, but the earliest mention of a choir of boys and men comes from 1127 and it was not until 1263 that anybody was appointed specifically to look after the children's training.

Over the centuries, the St Paul's choirboys became famous and won a series of nicknames – Paul's Children, St Paul's Urchins and The Children of St Paul's.

Their popularity rose and fell as politics and the national mood changed. In the 16th century, they branched out into drama and became one of Elizabeth I's favourite acting troupes, performing at royal palaces in the evenings and returning by boat along the River Thames in time for their lessons the next day.

In the 17th century, opponents of the King tried to tear down the organ and banned the choir, which resulted in a shortage of trained singers after the monarchy was restored in 1660.

Wren's new St Paul's was a magnet to musicians of all kinds, who set up in the churchyard and were joined by music publishers and instrument-makers. They gave the first public concerts in England and supported the choir in oratorios – semi-dramatic pieces with religious themes.

By the 19th century, the need for proper schooling for the choristers had become apparent. In 1811, a formidable spinster named Maria Hackett decided that they should have a formal education. As part of her campaign, she attended every service at St Paul's for 60 years and visited other cathedrals to interrogate the apprehensive deans and organists. She lived long enough to see a new choir school finished in 1874.

The choir stayed in London throughout the bombings of World War I, winning praise for their courage in singing through the raids, but left for the rural safety of Cornwall in World War II. By 1947, they were back in London to celebrate the cathedral's 250th anniversary. Six years later, they sang at the Coronation thanksgiving service for the new Queen Elizabeth II and embarked on their first tour of the United States.

Since then, the school has moved to a new site to the east of the cathedral, admitted non-choristers and expanded to accept boys and girls aged from four to seven. In 1997, the word 'choir' was dropped from the school's title to reflect its changing role.

Around 110 children aged up to 13 and as many as 40 boy choristers are now educated at St Paul's, with the choristers' fees paid by the cathedral. Every pupil has music lessons but the choristers sing for an additional 22 hours a week, as well as recording CDs and touring the world. In the last ten years they have been to Brazil, France, Holland, Japan, Spain and the US. Some boys have been talent-spotted for opera and theatre productions. Others record CDs of their own and appear on television.

Today, the music at St Paul's, with its continuing tradition of innovation and inspiration, is the envy of other churches around the world. When the Archbishop of Paris was investigating the possibility of re-establishing Notre Dame Choir School, he chose St Paul's School as the best possible model.

*Opposite page*
Members of the St Paul's choir (Easter 1995)

*This page*
Top:     Choristers receiving musical tuition
*Bottom*: Advent Sunday 1997

### CARRYING A TUNE

*A brave employee managed to save 'three burdens of choir books' from the Great Fire of 1666. They weighed almost 131 pounds (60 kilos) – the current repertoire weighs several tonnes and could not be evacuated by one person.*

# The Friends of St Paul's

Fire had destroyed Old St Paul's and several of its predecessors. When raids on London began during World War I, a group of men and women who loved the current cathedral were determined that history should not repeat itself.

They therefore formed the St Paul's Fire Watch and patrolled the building to ensure that every stray spark from the conflict was extinguished before it could do any harm. They re-formed during World War II, inviting their friends and families to join them. After a public appeal, there were 300 volunteers, 40 of whom guarded the cathedral each night.

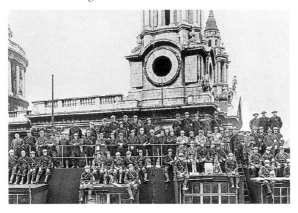

Mary Prendergast, who joined the Watch in 1939, remembers the problems of patrolling 'such an enormous building, with many complex avenues on the roof; corners and crannies - there could be an incendiary bomb anywhere in a small crevice, or under some masonry. If this was not promptly removed, it could....[cause] a fire well into the building.'

The Watch was disbanded at the end of the war but its members, who had proved their commitment in a time of acute danger, still wanted to do something to help the cathedral. In 1952, they therefore formed the Friends of St Paul's, with the Queen Mother as their patron.

Today, there are 4,000 Friends, who provide both financial and practical support. Half are from the UK, the others come from around the world, including Africa, the Americas, Australia, Europe, Japan and New Zealand.

Subscriptions are normally used for specific projects, such as printing the service sheets. Around 130 Friends who live near the cathedral have also become Working Friends, giving their time to welcome visitors, sell guide books and answer visitors' questions. A few of these become guides, taking a six-month training course and passing an examination before they start work. There are normally between eight and 15 Working Friends on duty.

Once a year, the Friends hold a one-day festival, which includes an early evening service and a recital by the choristers, usually in the presence of the Queen Mother. They also get free access to St Paul's, advance notice of cathedral events, an annual magazine and two newsletters a year about the cathedral and its work.

If you are interested in joining the Friends, please write to The Secretary, The Friends of St Paul's, Chapter House, St Paul's Churchyard, London EC4M 8AD, United Kingdom.

*This page*
*Top*: Members of the St Paul's Fire Watch
*Bottom*: The Queen Mother with the Dean and Chapter

*Opposite page*
The dome at night